FRANCIS FRITH'S

LONDON LIVING MEMORIES

THE FRANCIS FRITH COLLECTION

www.francisfrith.com

Francis Frith's
LONDON
LIVING MEMORIES

MARTIN ANDREW is an architectural and landscape historian and writer on outdoor matters; he is the Conservation Officer for Wycombe District Council in Buckinghamshire. He specialises in the landscape of lowland England, and combines his love of history, landscape and architecture in his writing. Since 1978 he has lived in Haddenham in Buckinghamshire with his wife and children. He is a keen long-distance walker, and enjoys riding his motor cycle round the country lanes of the Chilterns. He was born in Doncaster, but spent most of his childhood in Ealing and Carshalton in Surrey. After university he worked for the Greater London Council's Historic Buildings Division, Buckinghamshire County Council and Salisbury District Council, before joining Wycombe District Council in 1990.

photographs of the mid twentieth century

Francis Frith's

LONDON
LIVING MEMORIES

Martin Andrew

First published in the United Kingdom in 2002 by The Francis Frith Collection

Hardback Edition 2003 ISBN 1-85937-454-9
Paperback Edition 2009 ISBN 978-1-84589-493-1

British Library Cataloguing in Publication Data

Francis Frith's London Living Memories
Martin Andrew

The Francis Frith Collection
Frith's Barn, Teffont,
Salisbury, Wiltshire SP3 5QP
Tel: +44 (0) 1722 716 376
Email: info@francisfrith.co.uk
www.francisfrith.com

Printed and bound in Great Britain

Front Cover: **Whitehall, The Horse Guards c1960** L1305100t
Frontispiece: **Hammersmith, The Bridge c1965** H387047

*The colour-tinting is for illustrative purposes only,
and is not intended to be historically accurate*

AS WITH ANY HISTORICAL DATABASE THE FRITH ARCHIVE IS CONSTANTLY BEING CORRECTED AND IMPROVED
AND THE PUBLISHERS WOULD WELCOME INFORMATION ON OMISSIONS OR INACCURACIES

contents

Francis Frith: Victorian Pioneer

FRANCIS FRITH, Victorian founder of the world-famous photographic archive, was a complex and multi-talented man. A devout Quaker and a highly successful Victorian businessman, he was both philosophic by nature and pioneering in outlook.

By 1855 Francis Frith had already established a wholesale grocery business in Liverpool, and sold it for the astonishing sum of £200,000, which is the equivalent today of over £15,000,000. Now a very rich man, he was able to indulge his passion for travel. As a child he had pored over travel books written by early explorers, and his fancy and imagination had been stirred by family holidays to the sublime mountain regions of Wales and Scotland. 'What lands of spirit-stirring and enriching scenes and places!' he had written. He was to return to these scenes of grandeur in later years to 'recapture the thousands of vivid and tender memories', but with a different purpose. Now in his thirties, and captivated by the new science of photography, Frith set out on a series of pioneering journeys to the Nile regions that occupied him from 1856 until 1860.

Intrigue and Adventure

He took with him on his travels a specially-designed wicker carriage that acted as both dark-room and sleeping chamber. These far-flung journeys were packed with intrigue and adventure. In his life story, written when he was sixty-three, Frith tells of being held captive by bandits, and of fighting 'an awful midnight battle to the very point of surrender with a deadly pack of hungry, wild dogs'. Sporting flowing Arab costume, Frith arrived at Akaba by camel seventy years before Lawrence, where he encountered 'desert princes and rival sheikhs, blazing with jewel-hilted swords'.

During these extraordinary adventures he was assiduously exploring the desert regions bordering the Nile and patiently recording the antiquities and peoples with his camera. He was the first photographer to venture beyond the sixth cataract. Africa was still the mysterious 'Dark Continent', and Stanley and Livingstone's historic meeting was a decade into the future. The conditions for picture taking confound belief. He laboured for hours in his wicker dark-room in the sweltering heat of the desert, while the volatile chemicals fizzed dangerously in their trays. Often he was forced to work in remote tombs and caves where conditions were cooler. Back in London he exhibited his photographs and was 'rapturously cheered' by members of the Royal Society. His

reputation as a photographer was made overnight. An eminent modern historian has likened their impact on the population of the time to that on our own generation of the first photographs taken on the surface of the moon.

Venture of a Life-Time

Characteristically, Frith quickly spotted the opportunity to create a new business as a specialist publisher of photographs. He lived in an era of immense and sometimes violent change. For the poor in the early part of Victoria's reign work was a drudge and the hours long, and people had precious little free time to enjoy themselves. Most had no transport other than a cart or gig at their disposal, and had not travelled far beyond the boundaries of their own town or village. However,

by the 1870s, the railways had threaded their way across the country, and Bank Holidays and half-day Saturdays had been made obligatory by Act of Parliament. All of a sudden the ordinary working man and his family were able to enjoy days out and see a little more of the world.

With characteristic business acumen, Francis Frith foresaw that these new tourists would enjoy having souvenirs to commemorate their days out. In 1860 he married Mary Ann Rosling and set out with the intention of photographing every city, town and village in Britain. For the next thirty years he travelled the country by train and by pony and trap, producing fine photographs of seaside resorts and beauty spots that were keenly bought by millions of Victorians. These prints were painstakingly pasted into family albums and pored over during the dark nights of winter, rekindling precious memories of summer excursions.

The Rise of Frith & Co

Frith's studio was soon supplying retail shops all over the country. To meet the demand he gathered about him a small team of photographers, and published the work of independent artist-photographers of the calibre of Roger Fenton and Francis Bedford. In order to gain some understanding of the scale of Frith's business one only has to look at the catalogue issued by Frith & Co in 1886: it runs to some 670 pages, listing not only many thousands of views of the British Isles but also many photographs of most European countries, and China, Japan, the USA and Canada – note the sample page shown on page 9 from the hand-written *Frith & Co* ledgers detailing pictures taken. By 1890 Frith had created the greatest specialist photographic publishing company in the

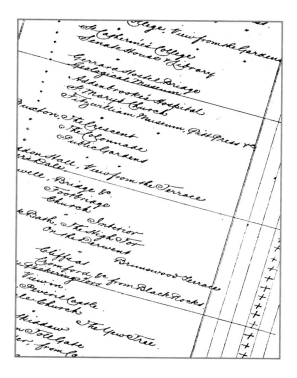

world, with over 2,000 outlets – more than the combined number that Boots and W H Smith have today! The picture on the right shows the *Frith & Co* display board at Ingleton in the Yorkshire Dales (left of window). Beautifully constructed with a mahogany frame and gilt inserts, it could display up to a dozen local scenes.

Postcard Bonanza

The ever-popular holiday postcard we know today took many years to develop. In 1870 the Post Office issued the first plain cards, with a pre-printed stamp on one face. In 1894 they allowed other publishers' cards to be sent through the mail with an attached adhesive halfpenny stamp. Demand grew rapidly, and in 1895 a new size of postcard was permitted called the court card, but there was little room for illustration. In 1899, a

year after Frith's death, a new card measuring 5.5 x 3.5 inches became the standard format, but it was not until 1902 that the divided back came into being, with address and message on one face and a full-size illustration on the other. *Frith & Co* were in the vanguard of postcard development, and Frith's sons Eustace and Cyril continued their father's monumental task, expanding the number of views offered to the public and recording more and more places in Britain, as the coasts and countryside were opened up to mass travel.

Francis Frith died in 1898 at his villa in Cannes, his great project still growing. The archive he created continued in business for another seventy years. By 1970 it contained over a third of a million pictures of 7,000 cities, towns and villages. The massive photographic record Frith has left to us stands as a living monument to a special and very remarkable man.

Frith's Archive: A Unique Legacy

FRANCIS FRITH'S legacy to us today is of immense significance and value, for the magnificent archive of evocative photographs he created provides a unique record of change in 7,000 cities, towns and villages throughout Britain over a century and more. Frith and his fellow studio photographers revisited locations many times down the years to update their views, compiling for us an enthralling and colourful pageant of British life and character.

We tend to think of Frith's sepia views of Britain as nostalgic, for most of us use them to conjure up memories of places in our own lives with which we have family associations. It often makes us forget that to Francis Frith they were records of daily life as it was actually being lived in the cities, towns and villages of his day. The Victorian age was one of great and often bewildering change for ordinary people, and though the pictures evoke an impression of slower times, life was as busy and hectic as it is today.

We are fortunate that Frith was a photographer of the people, dedicated to recording the minutiae of everyday life. For it is this sheer wealth of visual data, the painstaking chronicle of changes in dress, transport, street layouts, buildings, housing, engineering and landscape that captivates us so much today. His remarkable images offer us a powerful link with the past and with the lives of our ancestors.

Today's Technology

Computers have now made it possible for Frith's many thousands of images to be accessed almost instantly. In the Frith archive today, each photograph is carefully 'digitised' then stored on a CD Rom. Frith archivists can locate a single photograph amongst thousands within seconds. Views can be catalogued and sorted under a variety of categories of place and content to the immediate benefit of researchers.

Inexpensive reference prints can be created for them at the touch of a mouse button, and a wide range of books and other printed materials assembled and published for a wider, more general readership. The day-to-day workings of the archive are very different from how they were in Francis Frith's time: imagine the herculean task of sorting through eleven tons of glass negatives as Frith had to do to locate a particular sequence of pictures! Yet the archive still prides itself on maintaining the same high standards of excellence

See Frith at www.francisfrith.co.uk

laid down by Francis Frith, including the painstaking cataloguing and indexing of every view.

It is curious to reflect on how the internet now allows researchers in America and elsewhere greater instant access to the archive than Frith himself ever enjoyed. Many thousands of individual views can be called up on screen within seconds on one of the Frith internet sites, enabling people living continents away to revisit the streets of their ancestral home town, or view places in Britain where they have enjoyed holidays. Many overseas researchers welcome the chance to view special theme selections, such as transport, sports, costume and ancient monuments.

We are certain that Francis Frith would have heartily approved of these modern developments in imaging techniques, for he himself was always working at the very limits of Victorian photographic technology.

The Value of the Archive Today

Because of the benefits brought by the computer, Frith's images are increasingly studied by social historians, by researchers into genealogy and ancestory, by architects, town planners, and by teachers and schoolchildren involved in local history projects.

In addition, the archive offers every one of us an opportunity to examine the places where we and our families have lived and worked down the years. Highly successful in Frith's own era, the archive is now, a century and more on, entering a new phase of popularity.

The Past in Tune with the Future

Historians consider the Francis Frith Collection to be of prime national importance. It is the only archive of its kind remaining in private ownership and has been valued at a million pounds. However, this figure is now rapidly increasing as digital technology enables more and more people around the world to enjoy its benefits.

Francis Frith's archive is now housed in an historic timber barn in the beautiful village of Teffont in Wiltshire. Its founder would not recognize the archive office as it is today. In place of the many thousands of dusty boxes containing glass plate negatives and an all-pervading odour of photographic chemicals, there are now ranks of computer screens. He would be amazed to watch his images travelling round the world at unimaginable speeds through network and internet lines.

The archive's future is both bright and exciting. Francis Frith, with his unshakeable belief in making photographs available to the greatest number of people, would undoubtedly approve of what is being done today with his lifetime's work. His photographs, depicting our shared past, are now bringing pleasure and enlightenment to millions around the world a century and more after his death.

London - An Introduction

I SPENT most of my first twelve years living in West Ealing. I remember London's trams - my father took me for a ride on one of the last to run in central London in 1952. The trolley buses continued for some years more. My grandmother used to take me and my younger brother to visit London's museums; her favourite was the eclectic Wallace Collection in Manchester Square. My father took us to the Science Museum and the Natural History Museum, and we visited the National Gallery, the British Museum, the Victoria and Albert Museum, London Zoo, the Tower of London and Westminster Abbey. I have very fond memories of these 1950s trips. In those days the largest land mammal and the smallest stood in the main foyer of the Natural History Museum in front of Alfred Waterhouse's grand staircase - a pigmy shrew contrasted with the African elephant. And as for the blue whale suspended from a gallery ceiling, that was truly awe-inspiring to a young boy.

It seems such a remote world now. There were horse-drawn milk delivery carts, and you could hear the cries of the rag-and-bone men as their horses ambled by hauling flat-bed carts laden with junk. I went to school by steam-hauled suburban trains headed by 2-6-2 tank engines or by push-pull auto-car trains hauled by little 0-4-2 tank locomotives, while through West Ealing station thundered expresses hauled by King and Castle class locomotives. In 1953 we all gathered in a neighbour's sitting room to watch the Coronation on the only television in the street.

Outside my boyhood world, the later 1950s saw recovery from the economic doldrums after World War II, which had effectively bankrupted the country. There were bomb sites all over London. These were adventure playgrounds and informal nature reserves, full of buddleia and rose bay willow herb. The Festival of Britain in 1951 was intended as a new dawn, and the Festival Hall became one of England's leading concert halls. The Festival spawned an architectural style - and also a rather skinny furniture style that now looks somewhat laughable.

However, London was transformed by big ideas: social planning and the Welfare State. Architecturally this had little effect until there was sufficient capital to put these ideas into action. Councils embarked on major building programmes, sweeping away working-class terraced housing and filling the bomb sites with modern council housing in estates of varying scales. Work was plentiful in 1950s London: the Docks handled over a thousand ships a week, and factories were numerous, producing everything from buses to beer. As prosperity grew, and restrictions were lifted from office building and the development tax went, central London sprouted taller office blocks, many using the bomb sites - the City had suffered tremendous bomb damage. In the late 1950s office blocks also appeared in other parts of London, while schools and colleges were built or rebuilt in the new architectural style of reinforced concrete or steel frames with panelled infill. Indeed, public service architects led the way; some views illustrate the new style of architecture, for instance East Ham Technical College of 1959-62 (E100012, page 129) or the Marianne Thornton School of 1965-69 (C327056, page 112). Elsewhere comprehensive redevelopment, often linked to road improvement, produced spectacular change: a good example is Notting Hill Gate. Here a 1957 development plan led to road widening and comprehensive redevelopment, dominated by two high tower blocks, Campden Towers and Newcombe House (N164027 and N164028, page 58 and 59), both completed in 1962. These were towers of flats with shops on the ground floor - new housing was vital at this time.

It is important to remember that London lost a quarter of a million houses to German bombing; moreover, the country was too devastated economically and spiritually to rebuild substantially until into the 1950s. Estates of pre-fab housing, neat flat-roofed temporary houses, were built everywhere, and I remember visiting our home help's pre-fab in Ealing for tea many times: it seemed very cosy, and certainly had better heating than our own Edwardian semi in West Ealing. The London County Council led the way for new housing, and by 1949 had built about 50,000 homes in a conservative style, usually in four- or six-storey blocks with brick elevations. Very few private houses were put up until the mid 1950s, for property development took a long time to recover. The New Towns Act of 1947 was specifically aimed at re-housing Londoners in better, more rural conditions; towns like Harlow, Hatfield, Stevenage, Crawley and Basildon were planned, and grew up to absorb many Londoners.

The Festival of Britain in 1951 was a turning point. Optimism started to return. Then the Coronation of 1953 and the conquest of Everest led people to talk of a new Elizabethan Age; the De Havilland Comet, produced at Colindale and Hatfield, seemed a symbol of a modern, go-ahead country. Britain still considered itself a world power with a vast empire, but the Suez Crisis of 1956 both destroyed that illusion of power and encouraged the retreat from empire which had been started with the granting of Indian Independence in 1947. The Gold Coast was granted independence in 1957, the year after Suez, and Harold Macmillan's 'winds of change' swept the colonies to independence.

The 1950s also saw the beginning of coloured immigration from the West Indies and the Indian sub-continent. This greatly diversified British culture, but also imposed further burdens on the existing housing stock. Some run-down areas of London became dominated by the new immigrants, just as Kilburn had by the Irish years before. Brixton and Willesden are examples in this book, but not really until the late 1960s. By the 1961 Census, there were 78,000 people born in the West Indies in London, over 10,000 in Brixton alone, while there were 64,000 Asians from the Indian sub-continent. It has taken a long time to produce a multi-cultural society. Although things are better in 2002 than they were in 1962, we still have a long way to go. The point to remember is that London has always been a cosmopolitan city, and has derived enormous strength from different communities over the years.

In the mid 1950s London set about addressing social housing needs. All over London, Councils built taller and taller housing blocks. At first these were welcomed, as they had indoor toilets, bathrooms, central heating and decent kitchens - a contrast to working-class terraced housing, some of which was sub-standard. However, living in these tower blocks, which social planners and architects thought should be a paradise, soon palled, and we are still living with the legacy of this ill-advised phase of social engineering. But during the 1950s and 60s these blocks, incomplete interpretations of theorists like Le Corbusier, were seen as humane and progressive.

It is significant that the private developer, while he did produce blocks of flats, even sometimes tall ones, in the main carried on where he had left off before the War: estates of semi-detached houses proliferated from the mid-1950s onwards. Indeed, it is difficult to decide whether an estate of suburban semi-detached houses along tree lined avenues are 1930s or 1950s. However, the odd thing is that as house building got back under way, London's economy was changing, with major declines in manufacturing and the gradual collapse of the Docks as major employers. Many bemoaned this, but in fact the transition to a mainly service and commercial economy took up much of the slack. In the 1960s, for example, 'Swinging London' generated huge incomes for fashionable shops like those in Carnaby Street, off Oxford Street, and on the King's Road in Chelsea. The City remained the financial capital of the world, and colossal square footages of offices were built and rebuilt both here and elsewhere, in Westminster in particular. A good example is the Empress State Building in Earls Court, completed in 1962 (F69025, page 67). Tourism also helped - large modern hotels were built, often as tower blocks, like the Hilton off Park Lane, completed in 1963. Out to the west,

Heathrow Airport developed rapidly after 1955 and spawned a rash of architecturally varied hotels - one is illustrated at the beginning of Chapter 4.

Towards the end of the period covered in this book, the Greater London Council replaced the old London County Council in 1965; its boundaries included the whole of London's suburbs. Below the GLC were 32 London Boroughs - the GLC had powers of direction over them. Now there was a strategic authority over the whole metropolis, rather than areas controlled by counties (these were Surrey, Kent, Essex, a bit of Hertfordshire and Middlesex). Middlesex was abolished and subsumed within the GLC. Ironically, the GLC itself was abolished in turn in 1986, leaving greater London as 32 separate boroughs. Most of the views in this book are in fact within the area of the London County Council, which was formed in 1888. Exceptions are the Royal Docks and East Ham, both until 1965 in Essex, Crystal Palace just in Kent, and Ealing, Willesden and Heathrow in former Middlesex.

I hope this brief sketch of London in the 1950s and 1960s serves as a useful introduction to the views in this book. There is no denying that Greater London is a vibrant, creative and dynamic city; these views capture it as it changes from drab post-war austerity into a much more hopeful and confident state, partly demonstrated by the astonishing amount of building and rebuilding that took place. I hope you enjoy the views as much as I did, as I revisited parts of London I knew from boyhood and parts I lived in as a student at University College London in the mid 1960s, playing football and cricket in Regent's Park. I worked for the Greater London Council in the 1970s, helping to conserve greater London's architectural heritage, covering the City of Westminster and the former county of Middlesex. These selected views are a snapshot of two important decades in the history of one of the world's greatest cities, a history that goes back beyond Roman times.

The City of London and the Docks

St Paul's Cathedral from the River c1950 L1305003

Our tour starts at the heart of the City of London, looking towards Queenhithe dock with St Paul's Cathedral beyond. The river front is transformed since 1950. All the riverside buildings, then mostly warehouses, have gone, the last one only in 1996, replaced by commercial offices. Behind Frith's photographer, Shakespeare's Globe Theatre has recently been reconstructed. The coal barges were servicing the predecessor to the oil-fired Bankside Power Station, a building of the late 1950s, now the Tate Modern, linked across the river by a stylish footbridge.

The Tower c1950 L1305001

The City of London was defended by one of London's oldest and finest buildings, the Tower of London. William the Conqueror's White Tower keep, with its later jaunty ogee-roofed corner turrets, dominates the scene. Dating from the late 11th century, it is still the focus of the castle. The spring-foliaged trees hide the outer defensive walls.

The Tower of London c1955 L1305071

Down by the river bank, the paviours follow the line of the medieval wharf. Behind the moat are the medieval outer defences, the inner one overlooking the outer - the battlements are 19th-century. The projecting tower beyond the old cannon is St Thomas's Tower of the 1270s, which protected the river entrance, the famous Traitor's Gate. The Tower of London is probably England's most complete and historically-important castle, and fully deserves its immense popularity with tourists.

Tower Bridge c1955
L1305060
Frith's photographer stands beside Tower Pier (from here river cruises come and go), and looks south-east towards Tower Bridge. The buildings to the right have gone; the site is now occupied by the Greater London Authority building by Sir Norman Foster, resembling a gigantic circular insect eye peering at the Tower opposite. To the right is moored the World War II light cruiser HMS 'Belfast', a floating museum.

Tower Bridge c1960 L1305132

Nowadays an international symbol for London, Tower Bridge (designed by Sir Horace Jones) is a technical marvel, despite the Gothic-style towers. The bridge spans were raised hydraulically from their completion in 1894 until 1976, when they were converted to electricity. Work started in 1886 with extensive (and early) use of steel. The upper deck was intended as a pedestrian route, but nowadays it is a spectacular function room where you can watch the sunset over the Thames.

Tower Bridge c1965 L1305072

This view shows why Tower Bridge had to be built as it was: to allow tall ships to pass in and out of the Upper Pool of London. In this view, Tower Bridge's bascules are raised to the vertical, but they are rarely opened nowadays for shipping. Along the south bank there were wharves and warehouses into the 1970s, mostly now converted into offices and flats - or shops: Hay's Galleria uses Hay's Wharf buildings of the 1850s, 1861 and 1887.

The Port of London Authority Building c1955 L1305056
We head inland from the Tower of London to Trinity Square, where the Port of London Authority built its grand and monumental headquarters, starting in 1912 and finishing in 1922. It moved out in 1970, and the building became offices The PLA took over running the docks in 1908. To the right is Samuel Wyatt's elegant Trinity House of the 1790s, rebuilt internally after bomb damage; Trinity House run lighthouses and lightships.

The Docks c1965
L1305174
The Port of London held the key to Britain's stupendous 19th-century industrial wealth. The docks east of the Tower were excavated from 1799 onwards, becoming one of the industrial wonders of the Victorian world and even an attraction for tourists. Here Frith's photographer records the docks near the end of their life - many closed from 1967 on, the West India and Millwall in 1980, and the Royal group in 1981. Trade migrated east to Tilbury and its vast container port and to other more accessible ports like Sheerness.

◄ **The Royal Victoria Docks c1965**
L1305163
The biggest docks were the Royal group east of Canning Town on the north bank of the Thames. The Royal Victoria Dock opened in 1855, enclosing 94 acres of water. Following closure in 1981 and the establishment of the London Docklands Development Corporation that same year, all of the former docklands have been transformed with stylish flats, warehouse conversions, and office buildings. Canary Wharf is the most famous; its gigantic office tower, 824 feet (251 metres) high, was started in 1987, and now in 2002 has been joined by two others. The group can be seen from miles away.

Royal Albert Docks c1965 L1305169
The Royal Albert Dock was excavated in 1880 to the east of the Royal Victoria. It encloses slightly less water: 86 acres. To its south is the last Royal dock, the King George V, started in 1912 and opened in 1921, which encloses a mere 57 acres. Between it and the Royal Albert, London City Airport was built.

Royal Albert Docks c1965 L1305171
This view looks west from the A117 bridge, Woolwich Manor Way, past the entrance to King George V Dock on the left, towards Connaught Crossing bridge in the distance, which lies between this dock and the Royal Victoria. In front are Port of London Authority barges. As recently as 1956 the Royal Docks had been handling record volumes of cargo, so perhaps this is a good point at which to end this chapter, with the docks still bustling as they were within living memory.

The City of Westminster

Westminster Abbey from the South-East c1965 L1305277

Our tour starts at Westminster Abbey, one of England's finest medieval churches. This view is taken from the Victoria Tower above the royal entrance to the Houses of Parliament. Apart from the abbey, this view includes St Margaret's church (right) and the Foreign Office beyond. The trees in the middle distance belong to St James's Park. The skyscraper (far left) is the Hilton Hotel, completed in 1963.

Westminster Abbey c1965 L1305275
The west front of Westminster Abbey must be one of the best-known postcard views in England. The towers themselves are not medieval, as the rest of the great abbey church is; they were designed in medieval style by Nicholas Hawksmoor, and completed in 1745. The red granite and stone column is by George Gilbert Scott in lumpy Gothic mode, erected in 1861 to commemorate Westminster School old boys killed in the Crimean War.

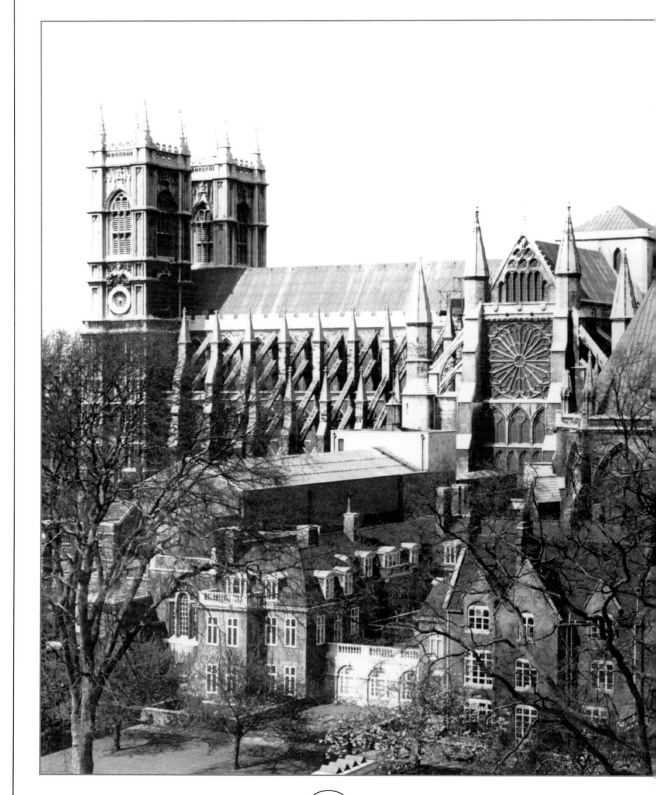

Westminster Abbey from the South-East c1965 L1305266
In this fine view of Henry III's great abbey church we see its main components: the 13th-century church with the 14th-and 15th-century left side of the nave, Hawksmoor's west towers, and at the right the lacy Henry VII Chapel. In the right foreground is a survivor from the medieval palace of Westminster, Edward III's Jewel Tower (the stone building with the round-headed windows). It was repaired in the 1950s, and the palace moat to its south and west was excavated: a fascinating glimpse of the old palace.

Westminster Abbey, the Nave Altar c1965 L1305262
We have entered the abbey at the west - this sequence of views goes from west to east, starting in the nave.
Henry III's abbey replaced the Norman one started by Edward the Confessor. Edward's choir, crossing and
transepts were complete at his death in 1066, but all was swept away in the 13th century. The pulpitum or
screen behind the altar is mainly 1828, and the monument in the left recess is to Isaac Newton.

Westminster Abbey, Henry VII's Chapel c1965 L1305257
At the far east end, behind the sanctuary, Henry VII's chapel was begun in 1503 as a rebuilding of the Lady
Chapel to take Henry VI's body. In the event, Henry VII's own monument lies beneath the soaring, lacy pendant
fan vaults of this most exciting and wondrously rich last flowering of the English Perpendicular style. Henry and
his wife's effigies are Italian Renaissance in style (by Pietro Torrigiani), an extremely early example in England.

Westminster Abbey, The High Altar c1965 L1305263

Through the pulpitum screen (L1305262, page 30) we enter Henry III's choir, with Victorian choir stalls on each side and the high altar beyond in the sanctuary. Purbeck marble is used for the columns and surface decoration: a rich, typically English Gothic effect. The columns and arches soar to the apex of the stone vaults 103 feet above the pavement. It is rare to see the floor as we do here, for the abbey is often shoulder to shoulder full of tourists.

◀ **The Houses of Parliament from across the River Thames c1955**

L1305301

A little further north along Albert Embankment we get this wonderful view of the houses of Parliament. Apart from Westminster Hall, the old parliament buildings were burned down in 1834 and the present buildings, in Gothic style, replaced them. To the left are the roofs and towers of Westminster Abbey. The riverside members' terraces now have awnings - red and white for the Lords and green and white for the Commons. At the left is the Victoria Tower, and at the right is Big Ben.

◄ **Westminster Abbey, The Cloisters c1965** L1305270
Because it was a royal abbey, the monastic buildings survived Henry VIII's Dissolution of the Monasteries. This view shows the south walk of the cloisters, rebuilt in the 1340s. Some of the walling on the right survives from the Norman monastery; this view shows this wall before a brutal restoration in 1970.

▶ **The Houses of Parliament and Big Ben c1965** L1305190
This view looks across Parliament Square, formed by Sir Charles Barry by clearing away houses, and re-designed after World War II. To the right is the 11th-century Westminster Hall, a survivor from the old Palace of Westminster, which was remodelled and given its wonderful false hammer-beam roof by Henry Yevele in the 1390s.

◄ **Lambeth Palace c1955** L1305069
Opposite and a little upstream of Westminster Abbey, the Archbishops of Canterbury have their London palace at Lambeth. It faces Albert Embankment, which was built out from the shoreline in the 1860s. At the right is St Mary-at-Lambeth, the former Lambeth parish church. In 1979 it was rescued by the Tradescant Trust and converted into the first Museum of Garden History. The Tradescants, father and son, were gardeners to Charles I. To the left is the late 15th-century red brick gatehouse to the Palace.

The Palace of Westminster from the Victoria Tower c1965

L1305279

The Houses of Parliament are on the right, and the ornate 19th-century south front of Westminster Hall is to their left. Beyond and across the road from Big Ben and to its left, the Victorian shops and offices have been replaced by the spectacular late 1990s Portcullis House designed by Michael Hopkins. We can also just see Nelson's Column at the end of Whitehall; to the right is the white stonework of the Ministry of Defence.

◄ **Whitehall, The Cenotaph c1950**
L1305019
North of the Palace of Westminster, Whitehall heads north towards Trafalgar Square. Once the site of a rambling royal palace largely burned down in the 1690s, the road gradually acquired government offices and the home of the prime minister in Downing Street - its entrance is just past the Cenotaph. On the left is Sir George Gilbert Scott's Foreign Office of the 1860s with the Cabinet Office of the 1840s beyond. The Cenotaph, the national war memorial and the heart of the Remembrance Day parade, is by Lutyens and dates from 1920.

◄ **Whitehall, Horse Guards c1960** L1305100
A little further north is Horse Guards, a fine building by William Kent of the 1750s and one of the earlier surviving government offices. Here we look east through the gates and across Whitehall to the Old War Office Building on the left, 1898-1907. The Lifeguards still mount guard here, their patience continually tested by tourists posing for photographs with them.

► **Parliament Square and the Jan Smuts Statue c1965** L1305265
Many photographs are taken from this viewpoint because it looks as if Epstein's 1958 statue of Jan Smuts, the South African soldier and politician, is peering at Big Ben, a shot rendered more difficult now by chestnut trees. The rebuilding of the Houses of Parliament to designs by Charles Barry and the passionate Gothicist, Augustus Pugin, took from 1836 to 1860. With the stonework recently cleaned, the so-called Mother of Parliaments looks fresh and continues to be a tourist magnet.

Whitehall, The Ministry of Defence c1965 L1305046
Leaving Whitehall, the photographer stands on the Embankment looking past Victoria Embankment Gardens along Horse Guards Avenue. On the left is the towering white Portland stone Ministry of Defence, designed in 1913 but only built and completed in the 1950s. The gigantic figures on plinths represent Earth and Water. Beyond is the corner of Inigo Jones's Banqueting House, begun in 1619, the only substantial remnant of Whitehall Palace.

Hungerford Bridge c1950 L1305002
The photographer looks at the south bank of the Thames, a scene now much changed - indeed, the Hungerford Bridge is the only survivor. Now concealed by a superb modern footbridge opened in 2001, Hungerford Bridge dates from 1863 and serves Charing Cross station. Beyond, the riverside with its cranes and wharves was swept away soon after this photograph was taken, for the 1951 Festival of Britain, from which the Royal Festival Hall survives. The tall tower was used for making lead shot. To the right of the bridge is now Festival Gardens and the marvellous London Eye.

Trafalgar Square c1960 L1305091
Back into Whitehall, our tour continues north to Trafalgar Square, which was laid out in the 1820s; numerous houses in front of St Martin-in-the-Fields church were demolished. It was named Trafalgar Square in 1830 even before Nelson's Column was built. The slope was dealt with by terracing the north part in front of the National Gallery in 1840.

Trafalgar Square, Nelson's Column c1960 L1305092
Nelson's Column is 170 feet (52 metres) high, topped off with the 17-foot (5.2-metre) statue of Admiral Nelson, the victor of the Battle of Trafalgar, still one of Britain's greatest naval victories. At the giant Corinthian column's foot rest lions by Landseer, added in the 1860s. The column is now screened off by low railings added in 1987.

Trafalgar Square, Nelson's Column c1950 L1305004
With summer sunshine catching the fountain, this is a delightful view of one of London's finest squares and still the venue for political meetings and rallies. This view captures a quieter moment with none of the intrusive road traffic that constantly circles the Square.

▼ **Trafalgar Square, the Fountains and the National Gallery c1950** L1305017
The two fountains were reworked in 1939 to designs by Sir Edwin Lutyens; the mermen and mermaids in greened bronze pour forth water to add to the fun. These are not quite as grandiose as the fountains in the Piazza Navona in Rome, but just as valuable in their energetic sculptural way.

▼ **Trafalgar Square, The National Gallery c1965** L1305185
The whole of the north side of Trafalgar Square is occupied by William Wilkins' National Gallery of the 1830s, its central portico topped by a dome. It has a long frontage, recently extended further to the west by Robert Venturi's ingenious Sainsbury Wing, in which classical columns and features gradually die out. Beyond is James Gibbs' wonderful 1720s church of St Martin-in-the-Fields, famous for its work among London's down-and-outs.

▲ **Trafalgar Square, The Fountains and Canada House c1950** L1305016
Here the photographer looks across the two fountains in their wide basins towards Canada House. New Year's Eve revellers and others on hot summer days frequently jump into the water. At Christmas time a giant Christmas tree is erected here, given annually by the people of Norway as a remembrance of British help in the Second World War. Canada House is partly 1820s, with more modern upper parts.

◀ **Cockspur Street, looking towards Trafalgar Square c1955** L1305040
This last view of Trafalgar Square looks past the Ionic portico of Smirke's Royal College of Physicians (now part of Canada House), and includes two other London icons: red double-decker buses. The building advertising Moussec and Philips, 1 Trafalgar Square, was the subject of a heated conservation debate in the 1970s; it was rebuilt in Italian Renaissance style in the 1980s, in the end to the benefit of Trafalgar Square.

◄ **Admiralty Arch c1960**
L1305096
The Mall was laid out for Charles II in the 1660s along the north side of St James's Park. It runs between Buckingham Palace and Trafalgar Square, and is screened from the latter by Admiralty Arch, built in 1911 as part of the memorial to Queen Victoria. To the left is the Doric-columned terrace of Nash's 1820s Carlton House Terrace; the monument commemorates the Royal Marines' role in the Boer War and China, 1899-1900.

Pall Mall c1950 L1305013

Part of the Trafalgar Square scheme included Pall Mall East, which was laid out to link it to Nash's Regent Street at Waterloo Place. This view looks past Waterloo Place towards the dome of the National Gallery in Trafalgar Square. The building on the right was the United Services Club by John Nash in the 1820s - it recently became the Institute of Directors Club. On the left, beyond the corner building of Waterloo Place (now Brasserie Roux and an hotel), rises New Zealand House, built in 1957-63, a 225ft tower block.

Buckingham Palace c1955 L1305050

At the western end of the Mall is Buckingham Palace, with the massive 1911 memorial to Queen Victoria designed by Sir Thomas Brock and Sir Aston Webb. Queen Victoria sits facing along the Mall, and the monument is crowned by a gilded figure of Victory. It is obviously more restrained than the Victor Immanuel monument in Rome, but to some tastes not by much of a margin. This is still one of the hot spots for visitors to London, particularly now that the Queen's picture gallery is open to the public.

Buckingham Palace c1965
L1305180

One of the most photographed buildings in the world, Buckingham Palace gained its frontage block by Sir Aston Webb only in 1913. This was actually a considerable improvement over Blore's reworking of Nash's 1820s mansion that survives beyond the main public facade. This is the Queen's principal London home, and thousands throng to see royal appearances on the central balcony, such as during Queen Elizabeth II's Golden Jubilee celebrations in 2002.

Piccadilly Circus c1960 L1305086 Piccadilly Circus was a key point in John Nash's splendid piece of early 19th-century town planning linking the former Carlton House with his new Regents Park via Regent Street. The Circus (in fact a triangle) now has at its centre Alfred Gilbert's wonderful Eros statue. All Nash's buildings have been rebuilt, including the County Fire Office (left) in 1924. The neon advertisements remain, but the pedimented London Pavilion theatre (right) has re-emerged as architecture stripped of advertisements.

The Devonshire Street Club c1960 L1305075
Further north, just off Marylebone High Street, stood the Devonshire Street Club, occupying a typical early 19th-century terrace house of the 'First Rate', according to the classes laid down in the 1774 London Building Act: that is, four storeys high and three windows wide. Unlike its neighbour, its first-floor window sills were not lowered at a later date. Unfortunately, in the 1960s it and its neighbour were demolished and replaced by a five-storey block. The building on the right, Elliott House, survives, and is now an estate agent's.

Oxford Circus looking North along Regent Street c1950 L1305009
Further north along Nash's Regent Street, a circus was formed where it crosses Oxford Street. In the distance is Nash's All Souls, Langham Place, finished in 1824 and a point de vue where the road curves left into Portland Place. This interesting view shows the spire truncated by bomb damage (since restored), while the building on the right was also destroyed by bombing and still not restored in 1950. Now renewed, it is identical with the other three blocks surrounding the circus, originally rebuilt between 1913 and 1928.

Regents Park, the Children's Boating Lake c1965 L1305230
Nash's great early 19th century urban scheme, his 'Royal Mile', led north to terminate in Regents Park. The Prince Regent, later George IV, was Nash's patron, and the park was formed from Marylebone Park, which had reverted to the Crown in 1811. Nash surrounded it with grand terraces of houses and laid out the bones of the park, including the lake. This view looks into the lake's north-west arm. The kiosk has now been replaced by the 1980s Boat House café.

◀ **Regents Park, The Restaurant c1965** L1305216
The next few views are in the Inner Circle, east of the lake, which had been leased to the Royal Botanic Society from 1839 until 1932. The Open Air Theatre soon followed, and in 1964 a stylish restaurant was built, consisting of a series of pyramidal and hexagonal pavilions. It is now named Queen Mary's Gardens Cafeteria, and is as popular as ever.

◀ Regents Park, the Canal c1965
L1305215

Nash's lake occupies much of the south-west quarter of the park. It is roughly Y-shaped, and curves parallel to the Inner Circle road. This view looks along the north-east arm towards the footbridge and a part of the lake now dedicated to wild fowl only. The stone end piers have since had their ball finials reinstated, and the rather utilitarian metal lattice balustrades have been replaced by cast iron balustrades.

▼ Regents Park, Queen Mary's Gardens Entrance Gates c1965
L1305238

When the area enclosed by the Inner Circle was returned to the park, it was laid out afresh as Queen Mary's Gardens in honour of the Queen and King George V's Silver Jubilee. A grand south entrance was provided via these ornate wrought-iron gates crowned by the royal cypher and the jubilee date, 6 May 1935.

◀ Regents Park, Queen Mary Gardens, The Island c1965
L1305236

Immediately north-east of the gates are the Island Rock Gardens, laid out in 1936. In the centre we can see the urn finial to one of the entrance gates. There is a bridge onto the island, and the gardens are interwoven with paths and rustic timber bridges. The gardens were restored in the 1990s, but look little different from their appearance in this view.

Regents Park, Queen Mary Gardens, the Sunken Garden c1965

L1305233

On the west side of Queen Mary Gardens is the Sunken Garden, planted by the Royal Botanic Society to exhibit geographical plantings until 1932. From then on it has been used for seasonal plantings; it is also known as the Begonia Garden, and in July 2002 was ablaze with begonias. In the centre is a fountain erected in 1936 with a crouching bronze youth sculpted by William Reid Dick. There is now a tall perimeter yew hedge.

▼ **Regents Park, London Zoological Gardens, the Polar Bear c1965** Z2015
As we cross Regents Park heading north, we see a curious miniature mountain range. This is London Zoo, and the revolutionary Mappin Terraces, built in 1914 in reinforced concrete to give animals a more natural habitat than cages. We can see part of them behind the polar bear. London Zoo, founded in 1824, was not merely a menagerie of exotic creatures, but was from the start devoted to the scientific study of animals.

▼ **Regents Park, London Zoological Gardens, the Elephant c1965** Z2018
When I was a boy, London Zoo was a favourite destination, but nowadays zoos are less popular. Perhaps the safari park experience has made people uneasy about captive animals. In fact, London Zoo pioneered this wide-open-spaces approach at its own Whipsnade Zoo in Bedfordshire, opened in 1931. In the 1950s I remember having rides on the elephants. Such a thing would no doubt be frowned on nowadays.

▲ **The Old Curiosity Shop c1950** L1305025
To conclude this chapter, I have chosen a photograph unrelated to our route as something of a curiosity. Just off Lincoln's Inn Fields, a small corner building is dwarfed by its neighbours (even more so now - the right-hand building has been demolished and replaced by nine-storey buildings of 1970). This building survives because it is thought to be the premises of Little Nell's grandfather in Charles Dickens's novel 'The Old Curiosity Shop'. This fame secured its survival; it now appears to sell clothes and shoes.

Westwards from Westminster

Kensington Gardens, the Peter Pan Statue c1965 K9008

This chapter heads west to Kensington and goes to Hammersmith and Fulham. We start in one of London's best historic parks: Kensington Gardens, now a continuation of Hyde Park. Together they form a park over two miles long from east to west. The 18th-century avenues, some garden buildings and the 1720s Round Pond survive in what is, by any standards, superb parkland. A more modern addition beside the Long Water is the statue of James Barrie's Peter Pan by Frampton, placed here in 1912, the gift of the playwright.

Kensington Palace, The Orangery c1965 K9002

At the western end of Kensington Gardens is the red brick palace
built for William III and Queen Mary in the 1690s and still a royal
residence. The orangery, probably designed by Hawksmoor and
built in 1704 in Baroque style, is an elegant building in which
orange trees in tubs and other exotica could over-winter. The
orangery is now accessible to the public, as it is 'open for light
refreshments throughout the year'.

Notting Hill Gate, Campden Towers c1965 N164027
The hamlet of Notting Hill, standing at the junction with Church Lane (now Kensington Church Street), was known as Kensington Gravel Pits, and only grew to its present size in the 19th century. There was a traffic bottleneck here by the 1930s, and in 1957 a redevelopment scheme swept away most of the old buildings. This and N164028 (page 59) show the results: two enormous towers, and blocks of flats over shops. This view, looking west along the north side, shows the 19-storey Campden Towers of 1962.

Notting Hill Gate, Newcombe House c1965 N164028
The other big tower is Newcombe House on the south side of Notting Hill Gate, also 1962 and part of the redevelopment plan. This view looks north along Kensington Church Street with a few of the survivors from the old Notting Hill Gate in the distance, including Lloyds Bank with the arched Venetian first floor window. Notting Hill Gate was considerably widened as a key part of the improvements.

Kensington, Holland Street c1965 K9011
Moving south we reach Campden Hill, north of the old village of Kensington and flanked on the west by Holland House and on the east by Kensington Church Street. Holland Street was once a lane leading from Church Street to Holland House, and was developed from the 1720s in a somewhat piecemeal way. This view looks west, with an early Victorian terrace on the right and the end of the grander Gordon Place terraces of the 1860s beyond.

Kensington, Holland Street c1965 K9012
Frith's photographer looks east towards Kensington Church Street in the distance. Most of the terraced houses in this view are 18th-century, including the one behind the tree with the pedimented doorway (far right). This is the Old House of 1760; the artist Walter Crane (1845-1915) lived here.

Kensington, High Street c1965 K9034

South of Holland Street is bustling Kensington High Street, the centre of the old village. Here we look east past the entrance to Holland Park. Holland Park House, started in about 1605, was severely damaged by bombs in 1940 and demolished in 1955-57. In the distance is the spire of St Mary Abbots, Kensington's parish church, rebuilt in the 1870s, its spire 195 feet high. Troy Court and Stafford Court (left) are massive 1930s blocks of flats.

Kensington, The Commonwealth Institute c1965 K9021

The Commonwealth Institute, with its forest of flag poles each flying the flag of a Commonwealth nation, occupies what was most of the southern end of Holland Park. Behind Silvia Crowe's landscape of paved terraces, trees and a pool is the exhibition hall and offices designed by Robert Matthew, Johnson-Marshall and Partners and completed in 1962. A good modern building, it is a splendid venue for exuberant displays by dance groups and musicians from Commonwealth countries large and small.

Kensington, The Geological and Science Museums c1955 L1305036
South of Kensington Gardens is the museums area, dominated by Waterhouse's Natural History Museum and the Victoria and Albert Museum. Between the two, Exhibition Road runs north past the Geological Museum of 1929-33 and the Science Museum, started in 1913 but mostly built in the 1920s. Behind the trees on the left is now a modern extension linking the Natural History Museum to the Geological, built in the early 1970s.

◄ **Earls Court, Earls Court Road c1965** E198003
The ochre and green faience underground station's east entrance was built in 1915. Over the arched windows is the legend 'District Railway, G N Piccadilly and Brompton Railway'. The west entrance, opened in 1937, is some 300 yards away, opening onto Warwick Road and serving the Exhibition Centre (E198014, page 66). Beyond the 1870s four-storey terrace (left) is the entrance to Trebovir Road, which features in L1305041 and E198018.

◄ **Earls Court, Earls Court Road c1965** E198022
Bisecting the terraces and squares of south-west Kensington, Earls Court Road links Kensington High Street and Old Brompton Road. This is the main shopping street; many shops occupy converted or extended houses (left) - the London Electricity Board is now a branch of Boots. The Midland Bank on the corner of Barkston Gardens is now a pub, the Blackbird. The underground station is in the middle distance on the left.

▼ **Earls Court, Nevern Square c1965** E198018
West of the museums area, we go to Earls Court through the terraces of south-west Kensington, which were developed between 1870 and 1890. Here the 1876 stucco and brick Italianate of Trebovir Road (right) gives way to the yellow and red brick Queen Anne revival style of Nevern Square, begun in 1880. The stucco corner house on the right is now the Oliver Plaza Hotel, its portico columns oddly dressed in granite slips.

◄ **Earls Court, Trebovir Court Hotel c1955** L1305041
These four-storey terraced houses of 1876 in Trebovir Road show the last phase of Italianate town architecture with channelled stucco ground floors and Doric porches, the upper storeys in brick with ornate stucco window surrounds, all crowned with heavy cornices. Templeton Place (right) is now linked by infill extensions. The Trebovir Court Hotel is now flats, Mary Smith Court.

Earls Court, The Exhibition Building c1965 E198014
For many years the home of the International Motor Show (in full swing here), Earls Court Exhibition Centre was the first permanent commercial exhibition building in London. Built in 1936-37 by an American architect, the frontage is in a heavy-handed Art Deco Moderne style, not dissimilar to 1930s cinemas. It has hosted a wide variety of events, from industrial and commercial to Billy Graham's evangelising rallies. The great hall behind was rebuilt in 1990, and the front elevation has been clad in vertical metal sheeting.

Chelsea, The Kings Road c1955 L1305037
The King's Road was famous for trendy clothes and antique shops; in the 1960s Minis and Triumph Herald convertibles cruised up and down, the pavements thronged with peacock-gaudy young men and women. This view pre-dates the Swinging Sixties, with echoes of a less materialist era: the Gothic-arched building on the right is the former Wesleyan Methodist Sunday School of 1903. The dome belongs to Antiquarius, the well-known antiques centre, and the vast block of flats in the distance is the 1930s eleven-storey Whitelands House.

Earls Court, Empress State Building, Lillie Road c1965 E198025
Empress State Building is situated immediately behind the Earls Court Exhibition Building - an access ramp can be seen at the far right. One of London's first massive office towers, this building was finished in 1962. Built for the Admiralty, it is over 300 feet high with 28 storeys. The cars do not exactly look Brave New World, however. In 2002 it is being completely refurbished and re-clad to bring it back up to date.

Hammersmith, The Bridge c1960 H387014
Our route now heads west into Hammersmith, its centre visible from the A4 Hammersmith Flyover of 1962. Until the 19th century Hammersmith was a rural backwater to Fulham, with fashionable terraces of Georgian houses at the Mall along the river bank. Hammersmith Bridge links Hammersmith to Barnes (behind the photographer), where St Paul's School, founded in 1509, moved in 1969 from its site since the 1880s east of the Broadway.

◀ **Hammersmith, The Bridge c1965**
H387047
This view shows the Hammersmith bank's suspension tower and the 'chains' in close detail. Two groups of four eyebar links are duplicated immediately below to sustain the vertical deck stays - some pretty massive spanners are needed here. There are architectural contrasts here as well: the ornate late Victorian Digby Mansions with a domed corner tower (left), with Thames Tower beyond, built in 1962 for United Distilleries, extended in the 1970s and re-clad in the 1990s.

◄ **Hammersmith, The Bridge c1960**
H387019
This view from the Barnes side shows well the massive scale of the ironwork and French-style ornamentation, which dwarf the 1920s K2 telephone kiosk. The bridge was built in the 1880s by Joseph Bazalgette to replace an 1820s suspension bridge. It underwent a major overhaul in the 1970s, and again around 2000. The tower block to the right is Henrietta House, a ten-storey block of council flats on the 1950s Caroline Estate.

▼ **Hammersmith, The Dove Pier from the Bridge c1960** H387003
Frith's photographer now looks from the bridge north-westwards. The Mall is on the right, and Hammersmith Terrace behind the flags on the Doves Pier, which the crowded pleasure launch is approaching. The factory (centre - its sign says 'Bemax for Athletes') and the factory chimney to its right have since been demolished.

◄ **Hammersmith, Furnivall Gardens c1960** H387012
Furnivall Gardens lie between the A4 and the river. The gardens were formed in 1951 from a World War II bomb site, and are a valuable 'green lung' for the traffic-choked centre of Hammersmith. The photographer looks south-west towards the Dove Pier from within the former site of the Quaker Meeting House and its burial ground, which stood here from 1765 until the 1944 bombing raid and are commemorated by the granite pillar.

Hammersmith, Furnivall Gardens c1960 H387004
Frith's photographer has moved nearer the river, and looks west towards Upper Mall, whose houses survived World War II. The stylish 1951 street lamps have been replaced recently by the ubiquitous fake period gas lamp standards favoured in refurbishment. The Dove pub nestles by the river amid mainly Georgian riverfront houses.

Hammersmith, Lower Mall from the Barnes Bank c1960 H387024
The scale of buildings with nothing over three to four storeys has now been rudely interrupted by the 1970s seven-storey extension to the Town Hall behind the 1930s brick building (centre). Left of it is the appalling 1960s Vencourt Hotel tower. At the right is the boathouse of the Furnivall Sculling Club, while the warehouse beside it (far right) was demolished for riverside flats in the 1980s.

Hammersmith, The Town Hall c1960 H387046
The cavalry exercising gently along the pavement would today find the wide dual carriageway of the A4 more of
a challenge. The Town Hall is a distinctive brick building with stone dressings finished just before World War II.
The pergolas to the upper terraces have gone, but otherwise it is unchanged. The view is from within Furnivall
Gardens, which were somewhat truncated by the A4 widening works.

Hammersmith, Town Hall Square c1960 H387010
Immediately north of the Town Hall there used to be a small park or square. This disappeared when the Town
Hall extension was built in 1971-75, its seven storeys uncompromisingly at odds with the old town hall building:
architectural bad manners or boldly innovative, depending on your point of view. Beyond is King Street, where
the single-storey gabled building went in the 1990s for a four-storey neo-Georgian building.

Hammersmith, King Street c1960 H387002
Frith's photographer was on the roof of the 1936 Cannon cinema, now a UGC cinema, looking north-east towards Hammersmith Broadway. The buildings on the left have lost their gables since the 1960s, and the Lilliputian two-storey building to their right was replaced in 1999. The foreground is occupied by the 1970s Town Hall extension. The domed building survives, but is no longer a billiard hall. In the background the new Hammersmith rises, including the scaffolding for Thames Tower (right) - completed in H387047 (page 70).

▼ **Hammersmith, King Street c1960** H387028
The photographer looks south-west from upstairs in the Art Deco building, occupied today by Kentucky Fried Chicken, past the entrance to Cambridge Grove, just beyond the Volkswagen Beetle car. The 1950s three-storey block (left) survives, but the one in the distance has been replaced by a five-storey 1990s building used by the social services. The three-gabled 1890s pub advertising 'Charrington's Entire' (left) is being refurbished as a theme bar.

▼ **Hammersmith, Ravenscourt Park c1960** H387023
Once the grounds of Palingswick Manor, Ravenscourt Park became a public park in 1887 - some of the layout is early 19th-century. It is still popular: when I visited in July 2002 it was hosting a steam fair. The old manor house was bombed in 1941, but the 18th-century stables survive, partly used as a cafeteria. The lake is nowadays reserved for waterfowl only (probably fewer insurance problems for the Council: ducks' parents do not sue after accidents).

▲ **Chiswick, Chiswick House c1960** C318025
Built in the 1720s to designs by the estate's owner, the amateur architect the Earl of Burlington, this exquisite Palladian villa was derelict by the Second World War. Taken over by the Ministry of Works in 1952, it was repaired and the original side walls reinstated. It is now open to the public, along with the superb 18th-century landscaped grounds. This view looks from between the 1733 forecourt piers - they originally had sphinxes on top.

◀ **Chiswick, Turnham Green 1961**
C318003
Chiswick's main shopping and commercial area grew up in the 19th century along a main route out of London, shifting Chiswick's centre of gravity away from the riverside village. Turnham Green has older houses, Heathfield Terrace along its south side, and Christ Church arrived in the 1840s to serve the rapidly-growing Victorian suburbs. This view looks from the junction of the High Road with Heathfield Terrace past the war memorial towards the chancel and spire of the flint and stone-dressed Christ Church.

▼ **Chiswick, High Road 1961** C318004

This view looks in the opposite direction to C318003 along Chiswick High Road, with the turning to Heathfield Terrace in the foreground. Hidden by the lime trees is the magnificent red brick Roman Catholic church of Our Lady of Grace and St Edward, built in 1904. Burton's 1930s store (left) is no longer Burton's, and Goodbans beyond is now a Boots. Out of shot on the right is the Sanderson Wallpaper Factory by Voysey, restored and extended in the 1990s as Voysey House.

▼ **Chiswick, Chiswick Bridge c1960** C318015e

Chiswick Bridge still has a remarkably rural setting, with playing fields on the Chiswick bank and a cemetery on the Mortlake side. This bridge is concrete faced in white Portland limestone. Built in 1933, it now copes with infinitely more traffic than the appositely named designer, A Dryland, could have imagined.

▲ **Chiswick, The City Barge, Strand-on-the-Green c1965**
C318032

Further upstream, we reach a delightful riverside sequence of buildings: Strand-on-the-Green, separated from the river by a paved pathway. The City Barge is an extremely popular riverside pub still. Apparently from the 15th century the Navigators Arms, it was renamed in the 19th century - by then the Lord Mayor's state barge moored here in winter. The brand new houses beyond the man on the roof are Magnolia Wharf, completed only in 1963. The river curves away westwards to Kew Bridge.

◀ Fulham, Riverside c1960
F69016

We turn back downstream towards central London to pass through Fulham. This was the older part of what is now the London Borough of Hammersmith; here the Bishops of London had one of their country seats at Fulham Palace, their main residence from the 18th century until the 1970s. This view looks north-west along the riverside path which runs along the edge of Bishop's Park, the grounds of the former palace. In the haze on the left are rowing club boathouses on the Putney bank.

Fulham, All Saints Church c1960 F69010
Seen from the approaches to Putney Bridge, All Saints church appears medieval; in fact only the tower, built in the 1440s, escaped a Victorian rebuilding in 1881. The park, Pryors Bank Gardens, with its neat floral bed is now more natural - the bed is crammed with bamboo, shrubs and a few lime trees. Other trees have grown up, and this view cannot now be seen. The road between the park and the church leads into Bishop's Park.

Fulham, Pryors Bank Gardens c1960 F69013
This view looks west from the same viewpoint as F69010, past the half-timbered lodge built in 1900, towards Bishop's Park proper in the distance. Bishop's Park was opened to the public in 1893 and extended in 1894 to include these former gardens of Vine Cottage, which was demolished. The garden was re-laid out in 1953; the rather good sculptures here and in F69010 are by J Wedgwood. Nowadays the elaborate floral beds have gone, to be replaced by grass and a few shrubs.

Fulham, Bishops Park, the Open-Air Theatre c1960 F69017

Bishop's Park was extended in 1900 and 1903. At the west end, south of Bishop's Avenue, an open-air theatre was built in the 1950s. After early successes, it was vandalised and even set on fire on a number of occasions. It was demolished in the early 1990s - a sad reflection on certain of the Borough's inhabitants. We look south-west to the riverside railings, with the theatre stage and lights on the right. The site is now a skate park.

Fulham, Sir William Powell's Almshouses and the Memorial c1960 F69020

Church Gate runs from Putney Bridge Approach towards All Saints churchyard gates, with the war memorial gardens to its south. Their centrepiece is the memorial by Alfred Turner of 1921. The trees prevent us seeing the almshouses to the north of the lane from here today. Founded by Sir William Powell in 1680, they were rebuilt in 1869 by the noted Gothicist John P Seddon in a romantic and fussy style, richly adorned with cusped arches, colonnettes and statuary.

Fulham, North End Road 1964 F69027
North End Road is a busy shopping street running north from Fulham Broadway to Hammersmith; it now suffers from a lot of steel shop shutters. This view looks south-east past the junction with Sedlescombe Road. The gabled buildings are of about 1900, with green glazed brickwork to the first floor. Beyond are 1870s terraces of shops with flats above. Behind the camera is Clem Attlee Court, mid 1950s three-storey council flats.

Fulham, The Broadway c1965 F69029

From the river, with its richer architectural heritage, we go north-east to the former hamlet of Walham Green, swamped by 19th-century development as Fulham expanded and met Chelsea. This view looks south-east along Fulham Broadway, with Harwood Road on the right. Beyond the late 19th-century Midland Bank with its tripartite sashes, pedimented dormers and large clock is the rear facade of Fulham Town Hall. This part dates from 1904, and contained a concert hall. The Swan pub (right) is now called Bootsy Brogans.

From Heathrow to Hampstead

Heathrow, Fortes Airport Hotel c1965 L1305176

This chapter is a whistle-stop tour of outer north London from west to east, starting with the environs of Heathrow. The airport opened with a single runway in 1945. From these small beginnings Heathrow has expanded to one of the busiest airports in the world. To serve travellers, hotels grew up near the airport. This view shows Forte's effort of the early 1960s near the M4 junction and its spur motorway into the airport.

Ealing, The Mall 1951

E63001

Ealing was in Middlesex until the creation of the Greater London Council in 1965. Since the abolition of the GLC in 1986, Ealing, like the other 31 boroughs, is now a stand-alone local authority, its boundaries now much greater. This view, taken before the GLC existed, looks west from the Mall with its tall Dutch Revival shopping parade into the Broadway, with the spire of Christ Church in the distance. The building with the spirelet and elaborate gable was the cinema where I saw my first film in 1954 (a western) - it has since been demolished.

▼ Ealing, Christ Church c1950 E63013

A new parish church of 1852, designed by Sir George Gilbert Scott, was built to serve the new town centre. It has a strikingly tall spire, and still looks much the same. A notable loss is the trolley bus overhead electric cables, the trolley buses' source of power. The collector poles tended to come off on corners, and I have happy boyhood memories of the conductor cursing as he reconnected them. The trolley buses disappeared in the mid 1950s.

▼ Ealing, The Town Hall c1955 E63031

The expansion of Ealing began with the arrival of the Great Western Railway in 1838; the District Line followed in 1879, terminating at Ealing Broadway. Ealing grew to become an Urban District in 1894 and a full Borough in 1901. The Town Hall predates these events, dating from 1888; it is by the town's energetic surveyor, Charles Jones. Built in Kentish ragstone, it was extended at the right in 1930, and symbolises the civic pride and ambitions of the town.

▲ Ealing, New Broadway c1965 E63065

Looking towards Christ Church, this view gives an idea of the self-confident late 19th-century character of Ealing, again choosing Dutch Revival style. On the right are more austere flats over shops; beyond are further terraces dated 1905. In the distance (left) the dome and white walls belong to the famous Bentalls department store, now demolished and replaced by the Arcadia shopping mall in the 1980s.

◀ **Ealing, New Broadway c1965** E63064
We now move east to the junction of New Broadway with the High Street (left), with Lilley and Skinner's stylish 1950s shop on the corner. This is now Barratt's Shoes. The glazed-roofed arcade beyond and the shops and flats behind it date from 1905. On the right is Christ Church's churchyard wall and the Town Hall spire. To the left (out of shot) is the Ealing Broadway Centre, a massive shopping mall erected in the early 1980s.

Ealing, New Broadway c1950 E63004
Further along New Broadway, looking across the junction with Bond Street, note the trolley bus overhead wires and the telephone kiosks (left), a K2 behind and a K6 in front. The restaurant sign (left) belongs to the cinema, now owned by UGC Cinemas. The buildings beyond the Town Hall went for large offices in 1980 and became the Civic Centre in 1987: they visually overwhelm the Town Hall. This is the start of Uxbridge Road - its houses have been progressively replaced by office blocks.

Ealing, Uxbridge Road c1965 E63078

Further west along Uxbridge Road the scale diminishes: the streets to the south in particular are mainly artisan terraces. Late 19th-century two-storey houses and terraces converted into shops are interspersed with later buildings. The Coach and Horses (right) with taller offices behind is a bland 1950s example. Daniel's department store beyond partly occupies a 1950s flat-roofed building. The Prince Arthur pub (left) at the corner of Dane Road has had its 1919 buff terracotta elevations painted green - it is now Ashby's.

Ealing, Haven Green c1955 E63003

North of Ealing Broadway station is Haven Green, with Victorian villas on its west side and shops to its east. The north side is dominated by Haven Green Court with its green roof tiles, a massive wall of five-storey flats built in 1927-38 and aimed at the London commuter - the flats replaced a large house, The Haven. West from Haven Green the road leads to Castlebar Park, which still retains many of its mid 19th-century villas.

Ealing, Pitshanger Manor, Walpole Park c1955 E63009
When I was a boy, Pitshanger Manor was used as a public library, which I visited often. The villa was built in 1801-03 by the great architect Sir John Soane for himself. It and the parkland were bought by Ealing District Council in 1899, and the park was opened in 1901. There was a small zoo in the park. This view looks across the municipalised lake towards the rear of the villa. In 1955 it was still the Walpole Library; it was fully restored in the 1980s, and is used as a museum and gallery.

Ealing, The Green, the Grammar School c1955 E63025
The old village of Ealing was south of the Broadway, with the parish church beyond Ealing Green. There are several 18th-century houses along the edges of the green, which tapers south from Pitshanger Manor. On the west side, Middlesex County Council built Ealing County Boys School in 1913 in Queen Anne style. It is now part of Ealing and West London College. At the right are the walls to Walpole Park. Next door is St Mary's, one of the village's original 18th-century houses.

Ealing, St Mary's Church c1955 E63021
South of Ealing Green, St Mary's Road curves past the original parish church of Ealing. The medieval church of St Mary, however, was entirely rebuilt in the 1730s, and in 1866 to 1874 it was remodelled and enlarged by Samuel Sanders Teulon, known by architectural historians as a 'rogue' or 'wayward' architect. Looking at the west end and the massive tower in yellow brick with some stone dressings, we can see why. The interior is quite extraordinary. The 1886 lychgate seems conventional by comparison.

Ealing, Gunnersbury Park Lake c1955 E63041
At the southern end of Ealing (actually in Brentford, and from 1965 in the London Borough of Hounslow), Gunnersbury Park is a large mainly 18th-century park with the A4 and M4 to the south and the North Circular Road to the east. Nathan Meyer Rothschild, the banker, bought it in 1835, and added over 300 acres to the west in 1861, bought from the bishop of London. Rothschild called this lake the Potomac Pond, a reference to the American Civil War of the 1860s.

Ealing, Gunnersbury Park, the Museum c1960 E63051
After the Rothschilds sold the estate in 1917, a consortium of local councils bought 200 acres and opened it to the public in 1926. The mansion at the east end near the North Circular Road survived, although there were uncertain years in the 1970s. The 17th-century house had been demolished in 1802, and Rothschild remodelled and enlarged its replacement in 1835. Here we see the garden front, flanked at each end by pedimented archways, remnants of the house's 18th-century period. It is now used as a museum.

Ealing, Perivale Church c1955 E63010
South of the teeming A40 Western Avenue, built in 1934, and of the 1930s neo-Georgian Mullet Arms pub, and reached by a public footpath, lies the former church of St Mary, Perivale. This served a scattered hamlet, and is now surrounded by Ealing golf course, formed from fields along the valley of the River Brent. A small medieval village church with a white-painted weatherboarded west tower, it was declared redundant in the 1970s and is now leased by the Friends of St Mary's, who use it as an arts centre.

Ealing, Gunnersbury Park, the Temple and the Round Pond c1960 E63039
Nathan Rothschild enhanced the 18th-century landscaped park, and several garden buildings survive. The best is the Temple, the focus of the Round Pond to the west of the mansion, for many years used as a boating lake. The Temple dates from when George III's aunt, Princess Amelia, lived here in the 1760s. To the left is the 18th-century walled kitchen garden, now local authority nurseries and a garden centre.

Willesden, St Mary's Church, Church Road c1965 W453001
We go north-east to Willesden, an area mostly developed by the end of the 19th century with lower-class terrace housing which swamped the hamlets that made up the parish. Church End has little besides the church from an earlier rural Willesden. The church was founded in 938; the tower and much of the fabric is medieval, but heavily restored in Victorian times, while the bays in front of the tower were added in 1852.

▼ **Willesden, High Road c1965** W453008

The High Road links Church End to Willesden Green, the other main hamlet of old Willesden. Its growth accelerated greatly when Willesden Green Station opened in 1879; it acquired its own parish church, St Andrew's, in 1886, in the High Road. This view looks west into the High Road from Willesden Lane, with Walm Lane on the right. Willesden Lane is no longer remotely lane-like; the Underground station is on Walm Lane.

▼ **Hampstead, Rosslyn Hill c1955** H391032

This tour ends in Hampstead, still as fashionable as it was in the 1950s, and indeed in the late 17th century, when its spa water was popular. Rosslyn Hill is south of the High Street, the road descending from the heights where the parish grew up. Late Victorian development gave the area its present character. The Rosslyn Arms (right), now The:Bar, was rebuilt in 1869; the Dutch-gabled terrace beyond was rebuilt in 1890 as Dudman's Hampstead Borough Stores. Between them is the Unitarian chapel, rebuilt in 1862.

▲ **Willesden, High Road c1965** W453005

The eclectic nature of the main shopping street is clear in this photograph, which looks east past the Park Avenue junction (left) to the start of Willesden Lane. There were late Victorian houses amid the commerce - their front gardens are on the left, replaced in the 1980s by shops. The 1870s Italianate terrace (right) contrasts with the timber-frame effect of the gabled buildings (left), only twenty years later. There is even a bit of 1930s Art Deco in the far distance.

◀ **Hampstead, Keats House c1955** H391026

A diversion east through streets of late 18th- and early 19th-century villas leads to Keats Grove, the road renamed in honour of the poet John Keats, who lived here from 1818 to 1820 before going abroad to die in 1821. Wentworth Place, built in 1816, was nearly new when Keats lived there; his fiancée, Fanny Brawne, lived next door. In 1925 it became a museum. A branch library of 1931 houses a Keats collection (its gutter is just visible to the right).

**Hampstead, High
Street c1955** H391034
The architecture here is
a mix of Georgian
terrace houses and
grander Victorian ones.
In the distance is the
junction with Heath
Street and Fitzjohn's
Avenue. The
pedimented house
survives (right), but to
its left the three
Georgian houses went
in the 1980s for
Hillsdown House. The
1878 building beyond,
with the white-painted
wall, is now a Café
Rouge. The 1920s K2
telephone kiosk (left)
has been turned round.
A little further up on
the right is the turn into
Flask Walk, a reminder
of Hampstead's spa
period.

Hampstead, Heath Street c1955 H391008 From the High Street we turn right to ascend Heath Street, which winds towards Hampstead Heath. While the core of Hampstead village is remarkably unchanged since the early 19th century, this stretch of Heath Street back towards High Street owes much to 1880s slum clearance and road improvement, so Victorian architecture dominates in the foreground, Georgian beyond. The Horse and Groom on the right is a contrast to the Georgian cottages next door. The spire is that of the 1861 Baptist church.

◀ **Hampstead, Jack Straw's Castle c1965** H391072
The original Jack Straw's Castle pub was destroyed by bombs during the Second World War; it was rebuilt in the early 1960s by the noted Classical architect Raymond Erith in Georgian Gothick style. Battlemented and weatherboarded, it is a delight. When I lived in the area in the 1970s it was one of the most popular pubs in London. It is astonishing that it is now closed and boarded up awaiting conversion to flats.

Hampstead, The Memorial c1960 H391037

At the top of the hill Heath Street levels out, passes Whitestone Pond and leads onto the Heath. At the junction with North End Way (left) and Spaniards Road (right) is the war memorial of 1921 bearing quotations from Hampstead's illustrious resident, John Keats. Behind is Heath House, a five-bay Georgian house closing the vista from Heath Street.

Hampstead, The Spaniards Inn and the Toll House c1955 H391003

Spaniards Road cuts across the north part of Hampstead Heath, a straight 18th-century turnpike road; its toll house stands opposite the Spaniards Inn, where the road leaves the Heath. The toll house's survival is remarkable, as it has been a traffic bottleneck for years. It was restored in 1967 and received a Civic Trust Award. The inn is Georgian, and still popular. The founder of Hampstead Garden Suburb, Dame Henrietta Barnett, lived in the house beyond to the right.

Hampstead, Highgate Ponds c1960 H391053

The remarkable survival of Hampstead and Highgate villages owes much to the public-spirited Corporation of London. In the 19th century it bought large tracts of heath, woods and open country around London, including Hampstead Heath in 1866. Later additions included the Hampstead Heath Extension in 1905 and Ken Wood in 1924. The open space which Constable painted in the 1820s is thus little changed, and covers more than 700 acres of rolling heathland and woods.

▶ **Hampstead, Highgate from Parliament Hill c1965** H391050
From Parliament Hill, with its summit at 319 feet, we descend towards Highgate Ponds, a string of eight large ponds, now used mostly for wildfowl and fishing, but used for boating and swimming in the years of these photographs. Here we look down towards the former Bathing Pond, with Highgate village beyond. The spire belongs to St Anne Brookfield of 1853 on Highgate West Hill. Today there are longer views to Canary Wharf.

◀ **Hampstead Garden Suburb, Finchley Road c1955** H391020
North-west of Hampstead Heath, the Finchley Road divides Temple Fortune to the west from Hampstead Garden Suburb to the east (right). The suburb, founded by Dame Henrietta Barnett in 1906 and planned by Parker and Unwin from 1906 onwards, was a deliberate contrast to the sooty regimented Georgian and Victorian terraces to the south. Most of the development in this view is early 20th-century, with a red brick dormered Queen Anne-style police station of 1913 in the left middle distance.

South and East from Clapham to East Ham

Clapham, Clapham Common, the Pond c1955
C327009
We cross to the south side of the River Thames and start at Clapham. This was a village focussed on Old Town to the north-east of Clapham Common; houses spread around the common during the 18th century, much of it fashionable and for the well-to-do. Development in the 19th century swept Clapham up into London's grasp, but the Common survived - it had been turned from rough common land into parkland by 1800. Several of the ponds were infilled, but three were made into important elements of the parkland, popular in the mid 20th-century for model boating and fishing.

Clapham, High Street c1960 C327040
Clapham High Street heads north-east from the corner of the common. It retained a few Georgian and early 19th-century buildings, but those either side of the Ferguson Television advertisement (left) have since been demolished and replaced by a four- and five-storey 1990s block. The middle distance on the right is now dominated by the ten-storey office tower of 1968, Mary Seacole House, which houses Lambeth Social Services.

Clapham, High Street c1965 C327073
Further north-east along the High Street, Frith's photographer now looks back in the Clapham Common direction past Cato Road (left). To the far left is a curious building with a huge semi-circular pediment. Now occupied by Moxley Architects, it was built as the Temperance and Billiard Hall in about 1900. At this end of the High Street many houses survive; those on the right have single-storey shops in front.

Clapham, Maritime House c1960 C327059
Old Town and the streets around it form the core of historic Clapham, with the site of the medieval parish church of St Paul in Rectory Grove. It was rebuilt in 1815, enlarged in 1879, and in 1969 became a community centre. To the right of Maritime House is a terrace of three brick Queen Anne houses of about 1705, a high-quality and valuable survival. Maritime House of the 1930s now houses a Job Centre and the London Academy of Administrative Studies. To the left the Fire Station is being built.

Clapham, Clapham Common, the Long Pond c1955 C327034a
Frith's photographer moves on to Clapham Common; seeking human interest, he pauses at the Long Pond at the eastern end of the Common, looking from the opposite side to C327009 (pages 108 - 109). In the distance are the houses of Clapham Common South Side, some of which survive from the 18th century and more from the 19th.

▶ **Clapham, Clapham Common, the Children's Playground c1965** C327071
The Children's Playground is in a westward projection of the common. The houses of Clapham Common North Side, part of the busy A3 London to Portsmouth Road, are visible through the trees. Behind the photographer the traffic teems along Clapham Common West Side. The playground is still surrounded by its hairpin iron railings.

◀ **Clapham, Marianne Thornton School c1970** C327056
Clapham Common South Side, part of the A24 London to Worthing Road, once had many grand villas and 18th-century town houses, but relatively few remain. The Notre Dame Estate of about 1950 intruded, with London County Council housing and the Marianne Thornton School, fortunately screened from the common by mature trees. The school dates from 1965-68, and has recently become Lambeth College's Clapham Centre. Bizarre narrow arch-headed window units now replace the older glazing grids.

▼ **Clapham, Henry Thornton School, Clapham Common South Side c1960**
C327053
Around the corner in Elms Road (which retains many of its mid-Victorian villas) is the Henry Thornton School, within the same site as the Marianne Thornton (C327056) and also part of the Clapham Centre of Lambeth College. This is a straightforward piece of 1930s traditional school architecture under a Queen Anne-ish influence, entered from Elms Road through heavy security gates and watched over by closed circuit TV cameras.

▶ **Brixton, Town Hall c1955** B666027
Brixton's proud Town Hall, now part of the London Borough of Lambeth's administrative empire, dominates an area totally different from around Clapham Common. Working-class housing and slums of the 19th century gave way to London County Council housing estates in the mid 20th century; these swept away many of the older streets. From the 1950s the area became multi-cultural.

**Brixton, Town Hall
c1965** B666026
The Town Hall was a
massive statement of
Edwardian municipal
confidence when it was
built in 1906-1908.
The beautifully-
positioned corner
tower, a fruity Baroque
piece, has gigantic
figures symbolising
Justice, Science, Arts
and Literature
crouched below the
clock faces. This view
looks along the Acre
Lane north front past
the Assembly Hall with
its pedimented tower,
both added in 1938.

Brixton, Atlantic Road c1950 B666010
The centre of Brixton was treated in a cavalier fashion by the railway companies, whose 1860s railway viaducts march across it: the London Chatham and Dover (left) on brick arches, the South London Railway on a wrought-iron flyover (right). The girder bridge has since been simplified, and the shop fronts on the left have been removed to expose the railway arches. The octagonal turret is dated 1880.

Brixton, Station Road c1950 B666009
Frith's photographer has now moved slightly further north up Brixton Road to the other side of the brick viaduct; the market is in full swing, nowadays with many Caribbean vegetable stalls. The railway viaduct arches are now exposed, with modern shop fronts set within them. The London Electricity Board has been replaced by the Lambeth Building Society in its 1889 corner building (left). The Toby Ale sign and the buildings beyond have been replaced by the Brixton Recreation Centre of the 1970s.

Brixton, St John's Church, Angell Town from the South c1965 B666038
Angell Town was an estate of 1850s Italianate villas, mostly semi-detached, built on curving roads centred on St John's church, whose 1853 tower is crowned by four pinnacles. This view is from an upper balcony of Eldon House, one of the eleven-storey blocks of council flats built c1960 on the Loughborough Estate. Nearly all the villas have since been demolished and replaced by four-storey council flats in yellow stock brick. In the distance we can see the Houses of Parliament, the Victoria Tower and Big Ben.

Brixton, Wiltshire Road, Angell Town c1950 B666005
We are beside the left turn into St John's Crescent. The pillar box survives, and so does the 1850s vicarage in front of the church. The houses to right and left have gone, those on the right replaced by 1970s Angell Park Gardens. Many of the villas survive in St John's Crescent, out of shot to the left.

Brixton, St John's Church, Angell Town c1965 B666031
St John's Church, by Benjamin Ferrey, was completed in 1853 as the centrepiece of Angell Town. It has a fine Perpendicular-style tower with chequer-work battlements and elegant corner pinnacles. The 1850s houses between it and the photographer were demolished in the 1970s and replaced by a large council housing estate, Peckford Place. The lime trees in front of the church survive, and have matured well.

Peckham, Rye Lane c1955 P289001
Rye Lane leads south from the High Street towards Peckham Rye and its common. We are looking north. The buildings on the left, late Georgian (the pedimented pair) or 19th century, mostly survive; single-storey shops are built out where their front gardens once were. Most on the right went for the Aylesham Centre, a two-storey brick-fronted shopping centre. Dunn's in the distance on High Street has gone - there is now a striking new library and sports centre - but the building to its left remains, the Kentish Drovers.

▼ **Peckham, High Street c1950** P289601

Peckham lies north-east of Brixton. This view from the eastern part of the High Street looks east, with Clayton Road on the right. The left-hand corner block survives, shorn of its gables and re-windowed. Beyond is the police station of about 1900. The houses and shops beyond have gone, replaced by Camberwell Borough Council's vast council estate of 1957 to 1963 - no building is over seven storeys high. The buildings on the right went for road widening and the GLC's Clifton Estate.

▼ **Crystal Palace, The National Recreation Centre, the Stadium c1965** C207043

The centre of the Crystal Palace park was developed by the LCC as a National Recreation Centre from 1956 to 1964. This view looks north-east across the still new stadium with its running track, tiers of seating and roof on the left. In the middle distance is the high-level bridge which links the buildings and the two parts of the park to north and south. The large building beyond is the Sports Hall, which also contains three swimming pools.

▲ **Crystal Palace, The Lake c1965** C207052

South of Peckham, our tour ascends to Crystal Palace at about 300 feet above sea level. It was here that Paxton's great glass and iron buildings from the Great Exhibition of 1851 were re-erected from their original site in Hyde Park. Nicknamed the Crystal Palace, the buildings gave the name to this hill in Norwood. The Crystal Palace burned down in 1936, but the terrace upon which it sat survives. The park has two lakes - this is the Lower Lake at the south-east end.

◀ **Crystal Palace, The National Recreation Centre, the Hostel c1965** C207037
Residential accommodation was supplied for visiting athletes, as well as staff houses. These were built as part of the original scheme. A staff house is on the left, and the eleven-storey tower is the Hostel, now more cosily renamed the Lodge, built for athletes' accommodation. To its right, hidden by trees, is the dining room (C207038, page 124). The buildings are stylish and clad in vertical cedar boarding.

Crystal Palace, The National Recreation Centre, the Dining Room c1965 C207038
The dining room is to the right of the Hostel and linked to it by walls and the single-storey building to the left. It is a good example of 1960s architecture, and has worn well. It has a copper sheet roof which has weathered to green, a roofing material very popular with 1950s and 1960s architects.

Greenwich, Royal College Promenade 1951 G204010
Our tour now heads north-east to Greenwich to a much grander building. The Royal Naval Hospital, a counterpart to the Chelsea Hospital for soldiers, began as a rebuild of Greenwich Palace by Charles II in the 1660s, but it changed direction in the 1690s. The second pediment from the right is Webb's 1660s work. In 1873 it became the Royal Naval College; when that closed, in the 1990s it became part of Greenwich University. In the distance are the chimneys of Greenwich Power Station of 1902-10.

Greenwich, Wolfe's Statue c1955 G204029
South of the Royal Naval Hospital, Greenwich Park climbs to 155 feet beside Christopher Wren's Old Royal Observatory. To its east stands the statue of General James Wolfe, the Victor of Quebec, who died in capturing it from the French in 1759. The statue dates from 1930. It is now surrounded by paving. A railed area to the left has panoramic views over London to St Paul's Cathedral, the Millennium Dome and Canary Wharf.

East Ham, The North Circular Road c1965 E100005
We pass under the River Thames via the Blackwall Tunnel - the northbound side dates from the 1890s, an early project of the LCC, which was established in 1888. East Ham was in Essex until 1965, but since the mid 19th century very much a part of greater London. Here we approach East Ham's town centre along the busy North Circular Road, which seems in places merely a casual linkage of suburban roads. These terraces of neat Edwardian bay-windowed houses survive, and lead towards the Town Hall with its tower.

East Ham, General View c1965 E100034
We are looking north-west from the Town Hall tower across the Barking Road (the A124), and along High Street North. The Denmark Arms with the small dome survives, but the department store beyond with the clock tower has gone and is now merely a car park. High Street North is now entered via a steel archway inscribed 'East Ham Town Centre 1999'. On the right are the gables of a rather good terrace of Arts and Crafts-style shops with flats over of about 1900.

◀ **East Ham, High Street c1965** E100016
High Street North is a relatively undistinguished and typical London suburban shopping street: the exuberance of the Town Hall complex is forgotten. The Midland Bank on the corner of Caulfield Road (right) is one of their 1920s Classical-style single-storey buildings that add quality to many High Streets. On the left the taller Victorian brick buildings were demolished in the 1970s and replaced by bland flat roofed ones.

◄ East Ham, The Town Hall c1965 E100011

Like Brixton, East Ham made a powerful architectural statement by building a Town Hall redolent of civic pride. This ornate one in Baroque style with French and Tudor overtones was built in a hard red brick and buff terra cotta and completed in 1903. A public library was added in High Street South (right) in 1907 and a fire station in 1913, both in the same style.

▼ East Ham, The Technical College c1965 E100012

Opposite the florid Town Hall on High Street South, the modern era arrived with the East Ham Technical College, an eight-storey block by J W Taylor and built between 1959 and 1962. The concrete panels have since been painted. The building is now part of Newham College of Further Education - since 1965 East Ham is part of the London Borough of Newham. On the right is the 1904 red brick police station, in typical Queen Anne style.

◄ East Ham, Central Park c1965 E100008

The view looks north across Central Park, with the rear gardens of High Street South on the right. In the distance is the main block of East Ham Technical College, completed in 1962, and in the foreground is Doran Court, an eight-storey block of council flats by C H Doody, completed in 1959. The 'Brave New World' had arrived in East Ham.

East Ham, Central Park, the Monument c1965 E100007
Central Park lies immediately south of the town centre to the west of High Street South. It is surrounded by streets of neat late 19th-century terraced housing. At its south-east corner is the rather fine Portland stone war memorial of c1921 in Baroque style with an upper cupola and dome. This view looks across High Street South; behind the bus is Southchurch Court, 1950s council housing.

Index

FRITH PRODUCTS & SERVICES

Francis Frith would doubtless be pleased to know that the pioneering publishing venture he started in 1860 still continues today. Over a hundred and forty years later, The Francis Frith Collection continues in the same innovative tradition and is now one of the foremost publishers of vintage photographs in the world. Some of the current activities include:

INTERIOR DECORATION

Today Frith's photographs can be seen framed and as giant wall murals in thousands of pubs, restaurants, hotels, banks, retail stores and other public buildings throughout the country. In every case they enhance the unique local atmosphere of the places they depict and provide reminders of gentler days in an increasingly busy and frenetic world.

PRODUCT PROMOTIONS

Frith products are used by many major companies to promote the sales of their own products or to reinforce their own history and heritage. Frith promotions have been used by Hovis bread, Courage beers, Scots Porage Oats, Colman's mustard, Cadbury's foods, Mellow Birds coffee, Dunhill pipe tobacco, Guinness, and Bulmer's Cider.

GENEALOGY AND FAMILY HISTORY

As the interest in family history and roots grows world-wide, more and more people are turning to Frith's photographs of Great Britain for images of the towns, villages and streets where their ancestors lived; and, of course, photographs of the churches and chapels where their ancestors were christened, married and buried are an essential part of every genealogy tree and family album.

FRITH PRODUCTS

All Frith photographs are available Framed or just as Mounted Prints and Posters (size 23 x 16 inches). These may be ordered from the address below. Other products available are- Address Books, Calendars, Jigsaws, Canvas Prints, Notelets and local and prestige books.

THE INTERNET

Already ninety thousand Frith photographs can be viewed and purchased on the internet through the Frith websites and a myriad of partner sites.

For more detailed information on Frith companies and products, look at this site:
www.francisfrith.com

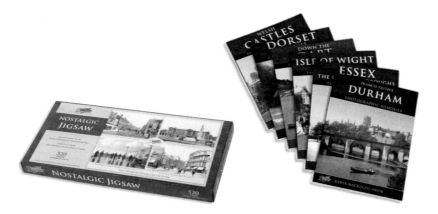

See the complete list of Frith Books at: www.francisfrith.com
This web site is regularly updated with the latest list of publications from The Francis Frith Collection. If you wish to buy books relating to another part of the country that your local bookshop does not stock, you may purchase on-line.

For further information, trade, or author enquiries please contact us at the address below:
The Francis Frith Collection, Unit 6, Oakley Business Park, Wylye Road, Dinton, Wiltshire SP3 5EU.
Tel: +44 (0)1722 716 376 Fax: +44 (0)1722 716 881 Email: sales@francisfrith.co.uk

---

See Frith products on the internet at www.francisfrith.com

FREE PRINT OF YOUR CHOICE

Mounted Print
Overall size 14 x 11 inches (355 x 280mm)

Choose any Frith photograph in this book.
Simply complete the Voucher opposite and return it with your remittance for £3.50 (to cover postage and handling) and we will print the photograph of your choice in SEPIA (size 11 x 8 inches) and supply it in a cream mount with a burgundy rule line (overall size 14 x 11 inches).
Please note: aerial photographs and photographs with a reference number starting with a "Z" are not Frith photographs and cannot be supplied under this offer. Offer valid for delivery to one UK address only.

PLUS: Order additional Mounted Prints at HALF PRICE - £9.50 each (normally £19.00)
If you would like to order more Frith prints from this book, possibly as gifts for friends and family, you can buy them at half price (with no additional postage and handling costs).

PLUS: Have your Mounted Prints framed
For an extra £18.00 per print you can have your mounted print(s) framed in an elegant polished wood and gilt moulding, overall size 16 x 13 inches (no additional postage and handling required).

IMPORTANT!

These special prices are only available if you use this form to order. You must use the ORIGINAL VOUCHER on this page (no copies permitted). We can only despatch to one UK address. This offer cannot be combined with any other offer.

Send completed Voucher form to:
The Francis Frith Collection, Unit 6, Oakley Business Park, Wylye Road, Dinton, Wiltshire SP3 5EU

CHOOSE A PHOTOGRAPH FROM THIS BOOK

 *Voucher* for **FREE** and *Reduced Price Frith Prints*

Please do not photocopy this voucher. Only the original is valid, so please fill it in, cut it out and return it to us with your order.

Picture ref no	Page no	Qty	Mounted @ £9.50	Framed + £18.00	Total Cost £
		1	Free of charge*	£	£
			£9.50	£	£
			£9.50	£	£
			£9.50	£	£
			£9.50	£	£
			£9.50	£	£

Please allow 28 days for delivery. Offer available to one UK address only

* Post & handling	£3.50
Total Order Cost	£

Title of this book . . . .

I enclose a cheque/postal order for £ . . . .
made payable to 'The Francis Frith Collection'

OR please debit my Mastercard / Visa / Maestro card, details below

Card Number:

Issue No (Maestro only):   Valid from (Maestro):

Card Security Number: Expires:

Signature:

Name Mr/Mrs/Ms . . . .

Address . . . .

. . . .

. . . .

. . . . Postcode . . . .

Daytime Tel No . . . .

Email . . . .

Valid to 31/12/12

Can you help us with information about any of the Frith photographs in this book?

We are gradually compiling an historical record for each of the photographs in the Frith archive. It is always fascinating to find out the names of the people shown in the pictures, as well as insights into the shops, buildings and other features depicted.

If you recognize anyone in the photographs in this book, or if you have information not already included in the author's caption, do let us know. We would love to hear from you, and will try to publish it in future books or articles.

An Invitation from The Francis Frith Collection to Share Your Memories

The 'Share Your Memories' feature of our website allows members of the public to add personal memories relating to the places featured in our photographs, or comment on others already added. Seeing a place from your past can rekindle forgotten or long held memories. Why not visit the website, find photographs of places you know well and add YOUR story for others to read and enjoy? We would love to hear from you!

www.francisfrith.com/memories

Our production team

Frith books are produced by a small dedicated team at offices near Salisbury. Most have worked with the Frith Collection for many years. All have in common one quality: they have a passion for the Frith Collection.

Frith Books and Gifts

We have a wide range of books and gifts available on our website utilising our photographic archive, many of which can be individually personalised.

www.francisfrith.com